KU-736-743

CATHY EKONDE

TOURISM DESTINATION MARKETING

A comparative study, between Gotland Island, Sweden and Limbe city, Cameroon

VDM Verlag Dr. Müller

LIVERPOOL JOHN MOORES UNIVERSITY
LEARNING SERVICES

Impressum/Imprint (nur für Deutschland/ only for Germany)
Bibliografische Information der Deutschen Nationalbibliothek: Die Deutsche Nationalbibliothek
verzeichnet diese Publikation in der Deutschen Nationalbibliografie; detaillierte bibliografische
Daten sind im Internet über http://dnb.d-nb.de abrufbar.
Alle in diesem Buch genannten Marken und Produktnamen unterliegen warenzeichen-, marken-
oder patentrechtlichem Schutz bzw. sind Warenzeichen oder eingetragene Warenzeichen der
jeweiligen Inhaber. Die Wiedergabe von Marken, Produktnamen, Gebrauchsnamen,
Handelsnamen, Warenbezeichnungen u.s.w. in diesem Werk berechtigt auch ohne besondere
Kennzeichnung nicht zu der Annahme, dass solche Namen im Sinne der Warenzeichen- und
Markenschutzgesetzgebung als frei zu betrachten wären und daher von jedermann benutzt
werden dürften.

Coverbild: www.ingimage.com

Verlag: VDM Verlag Dr. Müller GmbH & Co. KG
Dudweiler Landstr. 99, 66123 Saarbrücken, Deutschland
Telefon +49 681 9100-698, Telefax +49 681 9100-988
Email: info@vdm-verlag.de
Zugl.: Gotland, Gotland University, Diss 2010

Herstellung in Deutschland:
Schaltungsdienst Lange o.H.G., Berlin
Books on Demand GmbH, Norderstedt
Reha GmbH, Saarbrücken
Amazon Distribution GmbH, Leipzig
ISBN: 978-3-639-34752-4

Imprint (only for USA, GB)
Bibliographic information published by the Deutsche Nationalbibliothek: The Deutsche
Nationalbibliothek lists this publication in the Deutsche Nationalbibliografie; detailed
bibliographic data are available in the Internet at http://dnb.d-nb.de.
Any brand names and product names mentioned in this book are subject to trademark, brand
or patent protection and are trademarks or registered trademarks of their respective holders. The
use of brand names, product names, common names, trade names, product descriptions etc.
even without a particular marking in this works is in no way to be construed to mean that such
names may be regarded as unrestricted in respect of trademark and brand protection legislation
and could thus be used by anyone.

Cover image: www.ingimage.com

Publisher: VDM Verlag Dr. Müller GmbH & Co. KG
Dudweiler Landstr. 99, 66123 Saarbrücken, Germany
Phone +49 681 9100-698, Fax +49 681 9100-988
Email: info@vdm-publishing.com

Printed in the U.S.A.
Printed in the U.K. by (see last page)
ISBN: 978-3-639-34752-4

Copyright © 2011 by the author and VDM Verlag Dr. Müller GmbH & Co. KG
and licensors
All rights reserved. Saarbrücken 2011

CATHY EKONDE

TOURISM DESTINATION MARKETING

LIVERPOOL JMU LIBRARY

3 1111 01376 2743

WITHDRAWN

Table of content

1.0 INTRODUCTION

We would often hear statements like; ´I would love to spend my honeymoon in a beautiful place". "I hear people from that part of the world behave differently, I would love to see for myself". "My friend told me the weather there is good, maybe I should have that feeling as well". "My boss says business there is unique". "It has a magnificent display of nature; I would love to have pictures of that". Out of curiosity and many other reasons people travel. Movement from one place to another is becoming very common and increasing too. Nowadays many countries, be they big or small, popular or unpopular are being visited by tourists. The United Nation World Tourist Organization (WTO) defines tourism as `travel for recreational, leisure or business purposes´. The World Tourism Organization also estimated that 25 million tourists visited other countries in 1950 a number which grew to 842 million in 2006, illustrating a big interest in international travel. Then later, in 2008 it published an estimate that there were over 922 million international tourists, an increase of 1.9% from 2007. The World Tourism Organization (WTO) also forecasts that international tourism will increase at an average annual rate of 4.1 % and an average of 1.5 billion arrivals have been estimated by the year 2020. This is solely blamed on the present modern technology of e-commerce, which has allowed tourism products to now become one of the most sold items on the internet (WTO, 2010).

People therefore seem to have developed a rapid quest in visiting and as a result many areas are being visited. How then do visitors choose their destinations? There are many strategic locations in the world like islands, seaside cities, places with well known history, destinations that display a variety of natural features or reserves, those with political instability, and mostly those with completely different cultures. It's therefore amazing how visitors chose a particular destination to visit. On the other hand, the media and adverting plays a strong impact on visitor's minds. People are exposed to various images designed by marketers to influence their decisions about certain places and the various products that it offers in a particular captivating way. We would realize that to some extend pictures are shown to people so much so that it has made them develop interest which was not their primary desire (Solomon et al. 2006, p.15).

This thesis seeks to explore what visitors consider when choosing a particular destination to visit. Since people are constantly planning and travelling, decisions about these would thus reflect various reasons why they select particular destinations. At the same time a lot of ideas run through visitors mind their minds as they try to satisfy their desires in a particular destination due to variety. It's a wonder therefore how every individual would chose where his or her desire would be satisfied and what they would consider when making this choice about a particular destination.

However the decision to choose a destination for a visit does not stand alone, it revolves about smaller decision like; how to get there, when to get there and where and how to live there. The United Nation World Tourism Organization (WTO) clearly points out that there are other service industries are associated with tourism; examples include transportation services, like airlines, ships and taxis. Hospitality services, like accommodations which refers to hotels and resorts, entertainment venues, like amusement parks, shopping centres, casinos, variety of music venues and the theatre (WTO, 2010).

This research would be conducted in two areas, Gotland island of Sweden and Limbe city of Cameroon. These two areas have been chosen because of their national fame as major touristic environments. Their geographical location being in strategic destinations has attracted a lot of visitors within and the country and out of these countries as well. I would explore visitors views concerning these with the intention to find out what makes these destinations stand out in visitor's minds as they decide where to invest their time and/or finances.

1.1 Background

1.2 Gotland Island

Figure 1. Location of Gotland Island Sweden (Google images, 2010).

Gotland Island which is noted as a popular touristic destination is the largest Island in the Baltic Sea. Alongside its sandy beaches, it is also known for its fossils, medieval walls and churches. It also has small islands like Fårö, Gotska Sandön and Karlsö Islands. It is estimated that in the summer, 700 000 non gotlanders visit this destination either by flight or by ferry. This island has also been beautified with numerous cafe shops. Each year it follows a tradition of organizing a race round Gotland and several music festivals with international artists and something prominent of this destination is the folk dance. But with all these we cannot say Gotland is the most outstanding island in the world. Why then do visitors choose to visit this destination? (Google, Gotland Island, 2010.)

1.3 Limbe city of Cameroon

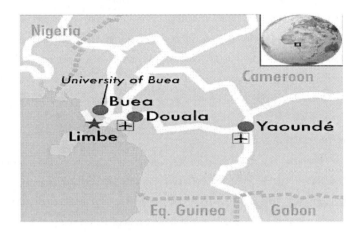

Figure 2. Location of Limbe city, Cameroon. (Google images, 2010).

Limbe city with black sand beaches as a result of petroleum reserves, appears to be the only English speaking city among three others that lie along the Atlantic ocean shores of the armpit of Africa . Formally known as Victoria, it was founded by a British missionary Alfred Saker in 1858, a history that still pulls visitors to the Alfred Saker's monument. It has a clear view of the Cameroon mountain and traces of the eruption that took place in 2000. The second best botanical garden in Africa is found in Limbe with various species of plants. Limbe also has a wildlife center with various animals. Many visitors go to Limbe almost every weekend regardless the reason of the year.

In 2009, it celebrated its 150 years of existence. However these characteristics or features do not make it outstanding enough, what then make visitors chose this area for a visit almost regularly? (Google, Limbe, 2010).

Using these two destinations I am on a journey to research the factors that trigger visitor's decision making as regards destinations to visit either at particular times of the year or at any other time of the year.

Cho (2008) said that an individual will be motivated to go somewhere if only they perceive their goal achievement; this however could be measured by desire which is a psychological wish of an individual. But Gunn (1972) also argues that without attractiveness a location will not invite visitors. However visiting a destination is an actual action that stems from a behavioral intention according to the theory of reasoned action. The theory of reasoned action emphasizes that a way of doing things by individuals, is related to norms under which they operate. Therefore people will always consider the consequences of their action before they make any decision (Cho, 2008).

1.4 Problematisation

There are many beautiful places in the world, what then could account for the choosing of a particular destination? Roe & Urquhart, (2001) point out that the tourism industry is volatile in nature and can be distabilised by other variables such as natural disasters, exchange rates in money and political reasons. These unforeseen circumstances are the things that could distort people's views on deciding where they should go. Ashley (2005) also suggested that the image of a place as being safe to visit is very crucial and could be easily damaged, thus could reduce visitor's interest to travel and confidence in a particular destination. I would assume at this moment that a visitor takes these into consideration when choosing a place to visit. Notwithstanding these uncertainties people are still making journeys to different destinations.

Visitor's satisfaction on the other hand which is very important requires some knowledge of culture by the host. Giuliani (1991), emphasize that when people's ethnicity, race and culture are mingled with those of others, their loyalty to this location could either be intensified or threatened. This is another factor that can hamper traveling especially considering religions where prayers are due at particular times of the day and particular foods forbidden. Choosing a place for any reason to visit would contain a bunch of factors. This research would explore the reasons that are crucial, and are highly considered by visitor when choosing a particular destination despite the complexities of language, time, religion and satisfaction uncertainties that exists.

This research could help the government of any of these countries develop its tourism industry. Here they could pick out the attributes that are considered necessary by visitors and try to insert them in their tourism industries. Local authorities or private individuals that are interested as well could use these attributes to adjust the destinations where they have their businesses to suit visitors, that is to say portray an image that is appealing to visitors. Some regions are already naturally beautiful and contain the necessary attributes but are not visited, this research could provide what is lacking to make this destination a chosen place by visitors for example like making the destination accessible and providing available information.

1.5 Research aim and question

This research seeks to evaluate what visitors consider when choosing a particular destination for a visit. I would love to find out the attributes visitor consider necessary prior to any visit, and what would inspire them to invest their time and money in a particular destination. This leads us to the following research questions;

What makes visitors choose a particular destination?

It would also include sub questions like;
1. What makes them satisfied?
2. What makes them willing to go back?

I would focus more on the first question which seems to embody the other two. Gotland Island or Limbe are not the most strategic destinations in the world today other places with quite distinct geographical locations exist. I have chosen these two places to conduct this research because I am a former resident of Limbe city in Cameroon and because I now study at the Gotland Island, Sweden.

The world has so many beautiful places, however despite their beauty, some of these destinations with more captivating locations are not chosen by visitors for a visit whereas they are close to them. What then qualifies a destination as potential visit area by visitors is the main interest of this study and I have decided to find out these reasons in two regularly visited destinations by locals and foreigners.

This research is also being done in a developed and a developing country would bring out different views and attribute that should be considered when trying to invest in any of these places, and evaluate if culture has an impact on people choices about destination decision choices.

2.0 Literature Review

2.1 Destination decision making and destination image

Visitor's decision about a destination to visit is associated with beliefs and cognition. These views about a destination, which plays an important part in the decision making process is a collection of ideas, beliefs and perceptions people have about the daily happenings in a destination and the attributes they attach with the destination (Lin et al., 2007).

This ends up in creating an image in an individual's mind about that destination (Echtner & Ritchie 1993). However studies conducted showed that stereotypes of images about a destination are reflected in the travel decisions. Pre-purchase impressions, and post purchase views formulate consumer's attributes towards a product. This can be called a stereotype of the destination's image (Lin et al., 2007).

In earlier empirical research, it was discovered that there exist a relation between what someone has in mind and their preferences in decision making. In the nut shell a destination's image does have an impact on visitor's preferences and final decision making. However not all destination images are built up from cognitive and affective conceptions do have an influence on visitors destination choices (Lin et al., 2007). But a lack of knowledge surely about a place would normally only give room for a more holistic perception (Jang et al., 2007).

2.2 Destination decision making and gender

Gender plays a role in the travel decisions. Males have been noted for traveling often as a result of work associated issues or businesses, while females on the other hand are noted for travelling more for recreational reasons. This means decision on destinations to visit could be reflected in gender. Gender is related to personality, visitor's way of acting and their intentions to go towards attractions (Meng & Uysa 2008).

Opposite views in socio- psychological intentions which represent push and pull factors that determine destination choices. These pull and push factors were analyzed on Australian leisure travelers from a gender point of view. Results from these indicated that there were differences in the gender decisions as concerns push and pull factors. Females were seen to make decision associated with culture, family bonding opportunities and ego while male's

8

LIVERPOOL JOHN MOORES UNIVERSITY
LEARNING SERVICES

decisions were related to sports, and new experiences when planning on destinations to visit (Meng & Uysa 2008).

The results also pointed out that females are more risk averse in their choices of destinations to visit and consider educational opportunities while males are adventurous or risk taking in their decisions. It also pointed out that males and females of the same age group could have different views as regards leisure destination choices. In business travels especially considering hotel choices and service delivery, women prioritized security, self service and lower prices as opposed to men who valued business services and things associated with more when making decisions (Meng & Uysa 2008).

2.3 Destination decision making and service intangibility

Clow *et al.* (2006, p. 404) explained that there is an imbalance in communicating the services associated with visiting a destination since services are intangible. This therefore urges the producers to have some aspect of physical asset that can portray quality. Traveling leaves memories for a life time and it's thus complicated to be promoted because of its intangibility. Decision making related to services are challenging to marketing as a whole. Pre purchase choices about services (traveling in this case) are more risky since it is not possible to touch or feel. Therefore tourist destination brand image is a major influencing factor in a traveler's destination choice (Bolan & Williams 2008).

2.4 Destination decision making and individuals

According to Fesenmaier & Jeng (2000) general studies about destination choices by visitors have been explored through various decision making channel processes. Coathup (1999) suggests that as people's knowledge widen about new things and areas, their desire for adventure, new opportunities and experiences also changes. These could be reflected in the choices they make about destinations to visit. Leisen (2001), claim that visitor's choices about destinations are related to their financial and time allocation. We can say that is quite logical but Jang et al. (2007) also identified that visitors decision about a destination to visit and collection of information depends on the stage of the family life cycle of the individuals concerned.

There is also the aspect of decision making associated with cognition. According to Lavidge & Steiner (1961) visitor's decisions stem from a hierarchy of effect which involves a cognitive level, affective level and behavioral level. An evoke set as Howard (1963) explains, is a collection of preferred alternatives of brands which consumers who in this cases are visitors group together as being necessary when purchasing any product.

A choice set on wider bases refers to the way visitors first of all view a brand or product and its alternatives and then analyze them together to come out with a decision (Decrop, 2009).

In addition to these, other studies too direct their focus on structure and size of the sets. We could see in this case that a list would be formulated with all the attributes considered as desirable by the visitor in his/her decision making process. This is just one view concerning evoke set because there exist another views as suggested by Decrop (2009) which are related clearly to theoretical and conceptual framework and do not have any empirical base. Thus the decision making here gently eliminates the number of alternatives, which is in the same light as a rational decision making (Decrop 2009).

Visitors in this scenario would do this elimination of alternatives as a result of low cognitive storage capacity, and ease information accumulation about different areas (Decrop 2009). To actually form an evoke set; retrieval (memory) is necessary. It constitutes of ideas to be considered, or places already known (Howard, 1963). From this comes an action set which is a function of heuristics (Jang et al., 2007). Decrop (2009) noted a brand awareness set ahead of the action or consideration set had been introduced. It stood for a perpetual stage where all known destinations by visitors come to mind (the awareness set.) But this however works in a hierarchy fashion. 'It is now a truism of marketing that brand awareness is a necessary precondition for choice'' (Nedungadi, 1990, p. 264).

2.5 Destination decision making and time

According to Korça (1998) residents behavior have an impact on the hospitality of a destination which intend influences visitors decision on a destinations as regards visits. All tourism activities are influenced to some extent by time. Truong & Henscher (1985) stress that time is an issue visitors must consider since it cannot be stored for future usage.

Papinski et al, (2007) who brought in a model of time –space prism in the world of English speakers, in 1969 pointed out that this time – space prism is made up of three constrains; Coupling; referring to people's ability to be at a particular place at a given time. Capacity; points to limitations in the mobility of individuals to carry out their activities and other little journeys.

Authority; it indicates giving only certain people the right to visit certain places. All these therefore play a role in the destination decision making process of most visitors.

Findings also by Papinski et al. (2007) suggested that work related issues are always planned before any other daily routines. This thus would obviously affect the destination choices.

2.6 Destination decision making and culture

Divergence in culture as well can influence visitor's decision. Lew (1987), indicated that differences in attractions can cause visitors to travel to other areas. Culture unfortunately as Jackson (2001) indicated was largely excluded as a crucial factor of a destination choice whereas long time ago Hofstede, (1980) had declared culture does affects visitor's decision on destination choices. National cultures also have been utilized to demonstrate an impact on the destination choices of visitors as well as their journey patterns, without keeping out their favorite activities. In a study, culture was confirmed to be able to distort travel choices (Ng. et al, 2007) and McKercher & Cros (2003), emphasize that culture constitutes a strong point for travelling thus should be considered as a strong drive.

Basala & Klenosky (2001) suggested that people are flexible to go to destinations where their languages are spoken. It was realized that religion too played a part in travelling since Muslim countries were desirable visited mostly by Saudi visitors. Henderson (2003) pointed out after a study that Muslims considered Muslim destinations safe for visit and westerners on the other hand considered western countries best for them to visit. It therefore brings out the fact that the closer the culture of a place to a visitor, the more likely would that destination be chosen, and the wider the cultural difference the less likely would the destination be chosen or the decision choice be that destination. Thus visitors are drawn towards people who behave like them or share the same attitude (Ng et al, 2007).

2.7 Decision making and information

Destination choice decision is a function of information available from different sources (Gartner, 1993). According to Murphy et al (2007) in recent studies, travelers that love risk and want adventure did not seek a lot of information. But those who feared risk not only gathered information but also considered particular vacations and lodging facilities. Information search depends on destination desires and the different stages involved in the traveling itself. This would probably lead to variations at each stage of the journey that is the to and fro planning of the journey (Murphy et al, 2007).

Word of mouth (WOM) has also been a very important source of information which has a special influence on older people. This idea was deduced by Fall and Knutson (2001) who conducted studies on adults who were 55years and above travelling for leisure in the state of Michigan, USA indicated that 2/3 of the sample used Word of mouth as their source of information. Word of mouth (WOM) was mostly gotten from family and friends and older people preferred to visual expressions of images, thus TV advertisement played more impact on their travel decision than radio adverts. The internet was rated second to word of mouth as a source of information. They still suggested that those who use the internet to gather information about destination visitation and the buying of its associated services where normally acquainted to the internet , educated and earned a higher level of income (Fall and Knutson 2001).

Previous studies undoubtedly showed that various information collection about destination visitations are related to visitor's actions and choices, but word of mouth seemed to be the basic source of information for many visitors gotten especially from friends and family (Murphy et al, 2007).

There are factors too that linked climate as attracting visitors to a destination which Hamilton et al. (2005) tries to analyze. Exploring studies conducted by Pike in 2002 on 142 questionnaires on perceptions of destinations images, they found out that there was a narrow link between destination decision making process and the weather condition of the place although he found an association with landscape. Hu and Ritchie (1993) also carried out similar studies and declared that natural features and the climate were of unique importance in displaying a destination and could pull people.

Therefore sun bathe and a nice weather were fitted in as attributes considered by visitors in choosing a destination to visit. There is increasing evidence which supports climates as having a neurological and psychological influence on vacation (Hamiltonet al., 2005). All ideas do not only point to reasons why visitor would choose a destination but also why they could avoid a destination. Bansal and Eiselt (2004) suggest that choice decisions can be affected by health, security, time as already mentioned then also by expenses and distance. The risk involved in the journey itself resulting from limited ideas, distorts visitor's decisions and makes them doubt the quality of service that would be available (Wong & Yeh, 2009).

Regarding the fact that some opportunities occur only at particular times, visitors can miss better travel opportunities if they do not buy in time but delay because of mixed feelings about these services due to its intangibility or because they require a service that will meet their needs (Wong & Yeh 2009). When risk is concerned in decision making, decisions often turn to be slowly made or avoided .This retardation in decision making is referred to as hesitation, and that individual fear should be seen is a potential factor that can play on visitor's choice of destinations to visit (Wong & Yeh 2009). Thus when visitors perceive risk, they can delay in their decisions (Dhebar 1996, p. 37).

We realize therefore that the decision to visit a particular destination by visitors is an aggregate of many factors. It touches several areas of any individual's life, his/her beliefs and to some extend his friends and family as we have seen in word of mouth source of information. There was also another interesting point referred to as ´´Word of Mouse´´. I found this quite interesting because it shows how globalization especially the use of the internet to portray the image of a place has had a strong effect on destination choices (Kristine de Valck. et al, 2009). The features chosen for display and adjective utilized to describe these destinations, or its related services really count. This has influence many people to go to destinations which they never intended to visit, although some have been disappointed after the visit to the destination saying it is not what they saw on the internet. Upon using the internet visitors see only what has been published and build up an idea or create an image only from these pictures and the adjectives used to describe them. There word of mouse too has also had people testifying online or on destinations websites how their experience in that area was wonderful. (Kristine de Valck et al, 2009).

Visitor's consumption process can be divided into three parts; the pre, during and post visitation (Ryan 2002). These parts are very essential for any visitor's decision making process.
The pre-visitation involves the image viewed by the visitors about the destination. A positive image accordingly would likely be promoting visitation, and a negative image would normally do otherwise.
During the visitation there is of course service delivery which is an intangible process, it is therefore important to display some tangible assets to portray quality in the services. This is because pictures are essential in conveying the image of destination, thus would influence visitor's criteria, values attributes and perception about a place (Smith & Mackay, 2001).

Post-visitation is linked with visitor's satisfaction. Visitors analyze their experiences after their visits to a destination; the aftermath is what is important. It is this effect that makes an impact on choosing a destination for a second time or recommending this destination as a positive word of mouth to either a friend or a family member (Fall and Knutson, 2001).

On the other hand (Solomon et al., 2006, p. 258), stress that there are five steps involved in any consumer buying process. I have decided to look at the buying decision in this case as making a choice on a destination to visit.

The steps would therefore include;

- Problem recognition; realizing that a visit to a destination is necessary for a particular reason depending on the individual's age, gender, religion or occupation.
- Information search; individuals explore all available possibilities either through word of mouth or internet about destinations that can meet their needs.
- Evaluation of alternatives; they then weigh out each destination according to their personal attributes and may be their time and money constrains.
- Product choice. Then finally a destination choice is made.
- Outcome. (post visitation) Visitors experience after their visit determines if they could by any means recommend this same destination to another person and this depend on satisfaction (Solomon. et al. 2006, p. 258-277). This process is illustrated in the figure 3 below.

Stages in Consumer decision making

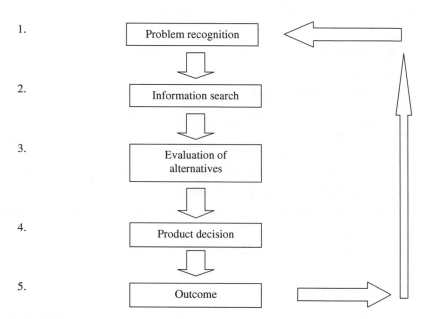

Figure 3. Stages in Consumer decision making. (Solomon., et al. 2006, p. 258)

According to Crick (1996) ´´Tourism is a social and economic phenomenon of profound importance in contemporary society.´´ Belk & Costa (1996), on the other hand say that ´´National governments, as well as regional and local authorities promote tourism destinations in order to drive economic growth and profit from its attendant benefits.´´ It is this promotion of travelling by the government and the society that has encouraged visitors to make various journeys around the world today. As people travel around the world they spend money. Lundie et al, (2007) emphasizes that tourism relates to the economic spending pattern of tourists which could either bring more, or less to the economy, it's an important factor because this reflects where and how visitors would be willing to spend their money. However the impact of visitors to a destination is well analyzed by the community, since it's the host country that feels the greatest impact in the industry (Korça 1998).

Lee et al. (2008) also talk about how celebrities to some extend have been involved in destination image displays. Some have even acquired contracts to show off a destination especially if they have a positive image and how fascinating a destination could be that they go there to relax or for business. This suggests why an image about a destination is very important because it affects choices in the decision making process.

Another most important point which is highly recognized in the studies of destination images is that conducted by Echtner and Ritchie (1993, 2003). It exposes three main levels of a destination's image. Firstly a destination image should be seen as having two main parts; an attribute -base and a holistic view. Secondly as they claim these parts have a tangible and an intangible component. And lastly a destination's image is made up of some general functional and psychological characteristics, or even peculiar events, ideas or feelings. This really demonstrated that an image creation in a visitor's mind is widely dispersed and cannot be pinned down to any particular attribute especially looking at these three levels of destination images by Echtner and Ritchie (1993, 2003).

3.0 METHODOLOGY

According to Fitzpatrick et al. (1998, p. 19-29), a research study could be conducted in two main ways; through a qualitative research and or a quantitative research. To analyze what makes visitors have particular interest in a destination so much so that they decide to visit it, this study would utilize only a quantitative approach to analyze why a particular could be chosen.

3.1 Quantitative analysis

Quantitative is an approach which uses figures or statistics and hard facts to explain or interpret particular behaviors. It cannot always say exactly why particular responses are given. It just uses the figures for data analysis. It is quite a simple approach which can give clean results. Thus it uses a deductive approach to conclude about valid results. Therefore for proper understanding the sample size has to be well explained. This kind of research also suggest a hypothesis be formulated that would be tested in this study. (Fitzpatrick et al., 1998, p.19-29)

3.2 Sample size and period of data collection

My respondents would be visitors of both Gotland Island of Sweden and Limbe city of Cameroon. The questionnaires were administered to Gotland visitors directly and those for Limbe were administered over the internet via electronic mail. A target of 100 respondents was set for both Gotland visitors and Limbe city visitors. No particular age group was chosen for this study as I intended to contact many visitors no matter their ages. Then I also tried to balance gender equality in each destination sample of which I had only a small variation in the numbers of males and females.

I used my trips with the ferry, ''Destination Gotland'' that transports people to and fro Gotland Island to administer these questionnaires. This was to cease the opportunity of encountering a variety of respondents and because everyone in the ferry would have or would be visiting Gotland island. I also choose to administer these questionnaires in the ferry to avoid getting into people's busy schedule which may cause them to give hasty results without reflecting due to time constrains. I randomly selected the visitors to in Gotland Island. The sample of visitors also included visitors, some of whom I happen to meet at Gotland University, others whom I met at a little gathering and later followed them up to administer the questionnaires. This was interesting because it gave me access to different category of people.

The visitors to Limbe city were contacted via electronic mail. I forwarded a copy of the questionnaire to visitors whom I already know visit Limbe, and also those who were recommended to me by visitors and residents of Limbe city. They therefore filled in the questionnaires and forwarded them back to me for proper analysis.

It should however be noted that although each destination's sample of visitors in this study were randomly selected, but generally respondents were not randomly chosen. This was to ensure each respondent was truly a visitor either of Gotland islands or Limbe city. Analysis of this research is based on responses of visitors on what triggers them to choose a particular destination. In later part of this research, a comparison has been made to evaluate the attributes most considered by visitors of each destination to know which are crucial in any destination choice.

The period of data collection was April 12, 2010 to May 10, 2010. This was done to enough time to encounter a variety of visitors especially to Gotland island and to allow Limbe visitors enough time to fill in the questionnaires and forward them back to me.

3.3 Questionnaire

The questionnaires used for this research were constructed using attribute suggested by Echtner and Ritchie (1993). Echtner and Ritchie (1991) pointed out that the image of a destination as seen by visitors could be measured using two methods, that is a structure and an unstructured method.

The structure approach made use of the of Likert scale technique to measure visitor's perspective on the points they consider before visiting any destination. Whereas in the unstructured approach, visitors expressed their opinions in a relaxed manner since they are allowed to voluntarily express their minds about the image they have of a destination.

I used the Likert scale of 1- 5 in the questionnaires. This is to evaluate the factors that have strong influence on destination choices, those that have neutral impacts and those that are not at all important in any destination decision.

The number (1) in the questionnaire stands for not being important at all, and its importance increases along the scale up to the number (5) which stood for a factor or attribute being a very important attribute thus has strong influence on visitors destination choices. There exist other types of ranges scales like the 3, 4, 5 or 7 of the Likert scale which I decided not to utilize since I deem it necessary to limit ambiguous answers and ease analysis (Robson, 1993).

Echtner and Ritchie (1993) emphasize that both methods, that is the structured and the unstructured methods are essential in any research that involves the way visitors view the image of a destination. The questionnaire constituted mostly of tangible attributes since it is very difficult to measure intangible aspects (Clow et al., 2006, p. 404). Therefore physical objects have been used to measure some attributes like service intangibility.

The questionnaire is divided in four parts. The main parts of pre-visitation, during visitation and post visitation by Ryan (2002), and the last part which is demography.
- Pre- visitation; this part was to measure how they visitors had information about this destination and how often they visited the destination.
- During visitation; here factors suggested by Echtner and Ritchie(1993) that have an influence on visitors' choices were meausured. They included: attractiveness of a destination, accessibility to the destination, accommodation, availability of information, beautiful buildings, business, climate, culture, fair prices, good local transport, history of the place, hospitality of the people in the destination, interesting local tradition, laws of this destination, many shopping opportunities, recreational places (bars, clubs and so on), safety in the destination, and unlimited access to areas in the destination. There was also an open question as to any other particular reason why visitors choose a destination. This open question was to give respondents a chance to participate in the unstructured approach of conducting destination image studies. Therefore they could voluntarily expressing their opinions as Echtner and Ritchie(1993) indicated.
-Post visitation; this part was to measure visitors satisfaction after visitation.
- Demograhpy; It was made up of the respondentts ages, occupation, gender, and nationality.
A sample of this questionnaire is represented in the appendix .

4.0 DATA COLLECTION AND ANALYSIS

Disposition

-I am conducting this research alone, however I have chosen to involve the readers in the analysis of this results, reasons why the pronoun, ``we´´ would be used in some parts of the analysis.

-This analysis is also testing the following hypothesis;

Hypothesis I; visitors consider particular attributes in a destination before they visit it.

Hypothesis II; some attributes are inevitable in any destination choice decision

4.1 Gotland Island analysis

As already mentioned 100 respondents were targeted. Each respondent took a maximum of 10minutes to answer the questionnaire and in cases where they had to express their opinion about why they chose this destination, the time extended to 15 minutes. However this was not so common since there was an open question which allowed personal gestures for the destination choice.

Visitors from China, Pakistan, Russia, Spain, Croatia, Ethiopian, Germany, Ukraine, Mexico, Nigeria, Latvia, Poland, Kenya, and also from within Sweden which constituted the bulk of this number were consulted.

This is illustrated below:

Nationality	Number of respondents (%)
Pakistan	10
Russia	3
Spain	1
Nigeria	6
Ethiopia	9
Germany	2
Ukraine	2
Tanzania	2
Latvia	3
Poland	2
Kenya	2
Bangladesh	7
Sweden	51
Total	**100**

Table 1. The number of visitors is and their dispersion towards each category.

From the table we can see that 51% of the respondents were Swedish. According to the responses in the questionnaires, I have constructed a table which shows visitors ratings toward each attribute according to gender. Then a mean of each of these attributes has also been calculated to show attributes influence on destination choices.The results are tabulated below in table 2.

Pre visitation

At the time of this research 24% of the visitors to this destination said they visited in the summer mostly. Others were here because of their friends and family which were about 51%, just 17% were here for education since they valued the quietness of the destination, and only 3% of the visitors were here for business reasons.

Knowledge about Gotland Island was mostly word of mouth and via the internet especially from foreigners.

| Attributes | Response from respondents | | | | | | Mean values |
| | Important (5, 4) | | Neutral (3) | | Not important (1, 2) | | |
	Males	Females	Male	Females	Males	Females	
Attractiveness of destination	40	48	-	-	7	5	4.2
Accessibilty to destination	27	36	10	18	2	7	3.8
Availability of information	32	36	10	18	3	1	4.0
Recreational places	56	24	11	9	-	-	4.4
Fair prices	30	42	15	13	-	-	4.1
Safety	25	25	24	26			3.8
Natural reserves/features	33	40	11	6	7	3	4.2
Laws of the destination	28	14	11	17	16	14	3.2
Unlimited access to places in the destination	17	21	6	2	28	12	3.2
Climate	13	13	19	21	22	12	2.9
Hospitality	36	42	-	-	11	9	3.8
Culture	20	51	9	10	-	-	3.9
History of the place	20	32	19	15	7	7	2.6
Business	12	18	15	15	21	19	2.5
Accomodation	38	36	8	18	18	--	4.1
Beautiful buildings	20	27	22	21	-	-	3.5
Interesting local tradition	22	11	21	23	12	8	3.2
Many shopping opportunity	36	40	10	12	1	1	4.1
Good local public transport	10	40	19	28	3		3.9

Summary of Gotland Island questionnaires: Table 2.

Looking at the table above, I have decided to consider only factors that have a total sum of over 50% in the important column of each attribute. This then indicates that only attributes with a mean value of 3.5 and above would be considered to have an influence on the destination decision and an extract is displayed in table 3 below.

Attributes	Mean values
Attractiveness of destination	4.2
Accessibilty to destination	3.8
Availability of information	4.0
Recreational places	4.4
Fair prices	4.1
Safety	3.8
Natural reserves/features	4.2
Hospitality	3.8
Culture	3.9
Beautiful buildings	4.1
Accomodation	3.5
Many shopping opportunity	4.1
Good local public transport	3.9

Table 3. Attributes that influence Gotland visitors.

From table 2, we can see that females loved attractiveness of destination, availability of information, and accessibility to the destination more than males. This supports studies by Meng & Uysa (2008) that females are risk adverse and evaluate a lot of alternatives before undertaking any journey, whereas males on the other hand are adventurous and therefore do not devote much interest into these factors.

Men instead happen to have chosen recreational places more than females. We can still assign this male attitude to their adventurous nature. As a result they would love to explore new areas and things that is why they valued recreational places more than females. It is interesting to note that females rated this same attribute 50% less than males. It is no more news that women are more price sensitive than men as illustrated in the results from Gotland visitors. However despite males risk taking nature as Meng & Uysa (2008) pointed out, everyone is concern about their safety. Thus men and women rated the safety attribute equally.

Other factors women considered more than men are culture, beautiful buildings and history of the place in particular which confirms studies by Meng & Uysa (2008), that women love educational activities. Women also valued good local transport than men. Could we say here that more men have cars than women? No because this would need to be investigated, therefore I would suggest that it is as a result of females loving comfort and considering they do not want to find themselves stock anywhere.

Post visitation

Many of these visitors said they would visit the destination over and over again indicating there were quite satisfied with their experience in this destination. They all indicated they would recommend this place to someone. They illustrated to have had information about this destination by word of mouth which they will continue to promote and just 25 % indicated to have had information from word of mouse, and 25% via the media. No one showed a choice out of wild curiosity. They all had some prior idea from someone or the internet before they decided to visit this place.

One particular visitor to Gotland Island said the place was quiet and good for studies in order to avoid distractions. An older respondent of 58 years said Gotland Island had a peaceful feeling since it is not so crowded, a reason why he keeps coming here. Thus he usually took off sometime every two months to Gotland Island to relax away from his family in Stockholm and border about the little business he had here at the Island to occupy him.

Demography

Although I tried to balance the gender issue, but males happen to have dominated the females Gotland Island. Males were 54% and females 46%. A suggestion for this is that it is not yet summer, a period when visitors abundantly visit this destination and therefore males being more business oriented as Meng & Uysa (2008)emphasized do most of the travelling at this time of the year. The gender category is tabulated below.

Age group	Number of respondents (%)
15-25	12
25-35	44
35-45	39
45+	8

Table 4. Age category of Gotland visitors

Looking at the table above, 25-35 happen to be the most active set of visitors since they are 44% of the total number of visitors to Gotland Island. Second age is 35-45, followed by 15-25. The last group of active visitors are those who are 45 years and above.

4.2. Limbe City

I also targeted 100 respondents for Limbe city and I got 113 respondents. This was because the questionnaires were forwarded by electronic mails and allowed respondents enough time to answer the questionnaires at their conveniences and recommend other visitors of Limbe city to me as well. However for the sake of equity in comparison, I streamed down the respondents to 100 to make it the same with the respondents for Gotland Island.

Most of the visitors of Limbe city are citizens of Cameroon, thus accounting to 70% Cameroonian citizens and just 30 % of foreigners. Then 14% were tourists, 6% missionaries and 10% scientists. Visitors are displayed according to their various nationalities below.

Nationality	Number of respondents (%)
Cameroon	70
Germany	9
America	6
France	5
Nigeria	1
South Africa	2
Ghana	7
Total	**100**

Table 5. Nationality display of Limbe visitors

A summary of questionnaires has been tabulated in table 6 below. This reports respondent's disposition towards each attribute.

Attributes	Response from respondents						Mean values
	Important (5, 4)		Neutral (3)		Not important (1, 2)		
	Males	Females	Males	Females	Males	Females	
Attractiveness of destination	28	33	12	10	12	5	4.0
Accessibilty to destination	36	42	11	4	4	3	4.1
Availability of information	20	28	11	15	6	6	3.4
Recreational places	43	35	12	9	-	1	4.2
Fair prices	35	41	19	5	-	-	4.2
Safety	25	33	28	14	-	-	3.9
Natural reserves/features	27	28	13	13	11	14	3.7
Laws of the destination	2	20	14	19	26	19	2.9
Unlimitted access to places in the destination	24	24	12	11	16	14	3.4
Climate	23	38	11	9	9	11	3.7
Hospitality	30	49	2	5	12	11	3.8
Culture	20	32	12	10	11	25	3.7
History of the place	21	20	11	11	27	10	3.2
Business	38	14	26	20	10	10	3.9
Accomodation	30	38	11	8	8	10	3.8
Beautiful buildings	11	12	13	20	20	21	2.6
Interesting local tradition	17	35	12	14	10	12	3.5
Many shopping opportunity	8	22	16	17	30	7	3.1
Good local public transport	35	25	6	11	14	9	3.6

Summary of Limbe questionnaires: Table 6.

Using the same method as in Gotland, only attribute with a mean of 3.5 and above are consider because the important column of the attributes sums up to and above 50%. These values are illustrated below, extracted from table 6.

Attributes	Mean value of responses
Attractiveness of destination	4.0
Accessibilty to destination	4.1
Recreational places	4.2
Fair prices	4.2
Safety	3.9
Natural reserves/features	3.7
Climate	3.7
Hospitality	3.8
Culture	3.7
Business	3.9
Accomodation	3.8
Interesting Local Tradition	3.5
Good local public transport.	3.6

Table 7. Mean values of important attributes of Limbe.

Pre-visitation

Since most of the visitors to Limbe were citizens of Cameroon. They had heard about Limbe as a town in the country while growing up. Some of them even had relatives here which gave reasons for their visits. But however they visited Limbe at least once every month for relaxation. Others like the scientists and tourists I can see were here because of natural features. Then the missionaries I would classify their reasons to visit under the religious part of culture since they came for church activities.

During visitation

Female visitors considered attractive too of a destination, accessibility to destination, fair prices, culture, hospitality, climate and interesting local tradition more than men. Attributes that showed a wide variation in gender were business and many shopping opportunities. Here men scored considerably higher than females. I would use my knowledge as a former resident of Limbe to suggest that men are considered as sole bread winners of the Cameroon society and thus are very tilted toward activities that generate income of which business is one of them.

Women on the other hand happen to be house runners thus ensure efficiency in household activities reason why there considered many shopping opportunities than men. This can be seen in their respective mean scores.

Unlike in Gotland Island, men rated good local transport more than females. We could be tempted after the reviewing results from Gotland Island to think that more females at this point have cars than men but, I would still suggest with prior resident knowledge that this is related to men's responsibility as main providers of the family and in cases of no personal cars they have no option than to rely on public transport.

Post visitation

They were also foreigners from Nigeria, France Germany and Holland who were in Cameroon for a visit and their business associates or 'friends recommended they have that ''fresh breeze eating fish experience, '' in Limbe city. Others were missionaries who came for Church activities or programs. But the bulk of foreigners constituted tourists like we have seen above who wanted to have some leisure time. They therefore came to observe natural features like the mountain and some animals they had never seen before. Scientists also happen to be visiting Limbe about the time this research was conducted. They were here to perform scientific experiments on some scare plants at the botanical garden in Limbe.

Most of the Cameroon citizens said they visited Limbe mostly to see family and spend leisure time with friends. They also pointed out that the town is busy throughout and safe for them at night therefore unlike other towns in the country were night time brought in fear of harassment. I can see from this particular point that this is quite a strong influence on visitor's decision to visit a destination. Thus if they perceive some uncertainty about their safety they would avoid these destinations.

Personal reasons

In cases where possible visitors would choice Limbe for business activities since it was close to them and they could relax in the town's comfort after work. Most of them indicated they enjoyed the fresh sea breeze since Cameroon is a tropical country with so much heat. They also indicated they enjoyed the fact that they could daily eat fresh fish along the beaches, roasted right in front of them which gave them the joy of belonging.

They also seem to love the local tradition of the people whom they say were quite hospitable a reason for this is that most of them are local business people and keep a good face to attract customers. They also said Limbe was chosen because it has fair prices in its product and services as compared to other towns in the country. The town was not so crowded and as busy as other major cities therefore traffic was absent. Motor bikes too where allowed in this city unlike others with which they could use to penetrate inaccessible or hilly areas. They also said everything was available in retail prices. They could get a small quantity of any product

28

LIVERPOOL JOHN MOORES UNIVERSITY
LEARNING SERVICES

without buying the whole packet. This made life less expensive, and comforting. Then based on familiarity they could have some products on credit.

Local public transport was very economical, they town was not so big they could move around on foot to the necessary areas to have fun. They also said language flexibility was unique and anyone could find their way around since English language is spoken or a local language called Pidgin English which could be understood by any average English speaker. Foreigners complained of insecurity since they were mostly of a different races and attracted attention. As a results sometimes there were exploited in service payments. They also feared pick pockets which was evident in cases of ignorance especially as they had to swizz together in the public transport buses or taxis with other people.

Demography

The ages of the respondents has been displayed below.

Age group	Number of respondents %
15-25	11
25-35	36
35-45	23
45+	22

Table 8. Age category of Limbe visitors

Form the table above it can be seen that the most active set of visitors are those within the age group 25-35 years, followed by 35-45 years. Those who are 45 years old and above happen to be more mobile than those who are in between 15-25 years old, therefore ranked third in the class of most mobile visitors age group.

All of the visitors were workers either part time of full time workers of Cameroon. The younger visitors that where in between 15-25 who are not working are students in different towns but come to the beaches in Limbe during weekends.

4.3 Comparison

The main similarity of this research is that visitors to each of these destinations at the time the research was being conducted were mostly citizens of these countries. This confirms facts pointed out by Basala & Klenosky (2001), that people tend to go to places where there exist less cultural differences from their own culture especially language indifference.

Looking at the tables, and reviewing each attribute in the questionnaire, it can be realised that factors like attractiveness to destination, recreational places are very important factors that determine visitors destination choices. Visitors to Gotland Island however considered these attributes more than Limbe visitors. Fair prices was also a major concern, but it was more valued by visitors to Limbe city than those to Gotland island. Variations in the number of visitors considering some attributes in one destination more than visitors in another destination could be assigned to differences in cognition which has led to behaviour.

Safety also constitutes a part of the destination decision, this can seen from the tables 1 and 2. Although climate was considered only in Limbe, because visitors to Gotland Island preferred mostly the summer season whereas visitors to Limbe visited almost every weekend due to the conducive weather.
Hospitality which generally had a more than 50% influence on destination decision is very important. The friendliness of residents in a destination encourages visitation (Korça, 1998).

Looking at the culture aspect which is very broad, I choose to narrow this down into two main parts. The first part is the food, drinks, religion and language part of culture in a destination and the second part is the way residents in the destination carry out their normal activities referring to interesting local tradition (Hofstede, 1989).
Visitors to Limbe therefore considered interesting local tradition more than Gotland visitors. As for the attribute many shopping opportunities which do not score enough points to qualify it as an influence on visitors destination decision, I however detected from the results that; it was of lesser importance to Gotland visitors than Limbe visitors.

Talking about the attribute good local transport, from the values of the mean in the table 2 and 6, it is clear that Limbe visitors considered this point more than Gotland visitors. Having been a resident of these two destinations, I would suggest that most visitors to Limbe do not have personal cars and therefore depended more on public transport than Gotland visitors. This suggestion arises from observations in my trips taken with the ferry "destination Gotland" that transported Gotland visitors because I realised many visitors to the island were on board with their vehicles.

Visitors to Limbe visit this destination as a result of prior knowledge from birth about this place. This indicates Limbe city is not as internationally recognized as touristic destination as Gotland Island, although its serves this purpose for its countrymen.

The visitors to Limbe have grown to know about its features and all the activities that go on there and do not need to search a lot of information from the internet especially regarding accommodation since they can find an available and affordable place on arrival. The visitors of Limbe tend to rely on word of mouth for directives to go around the town. Some visitors say information on the internet is not sufficient enough to know about this destination. There is always a number to contact service personnel for more information. I can deduce from this point that the manager concerned here tries to utilize a marketing strategy to create a customer relationship with prospective customers.

However visitors to Gotland Island considered information availability as a very important factor and accommodation preferences before undertaking any journey. This concludes visitor to Gotland Island go through more affective or cognitive processing to choose a destination than visitors to Limbe city who would involve less of affective and cognitive processing in their destination decision choices. Both males and females of Limbe city considered fair prices more in their destination choices whereas female visitors to Gotland Island considered fair prices more than the male visitors.

Based on the tables 2 and 6, factors or attributes that have a strong influence on destination choices in both Gotland Island and Limbe city have been extracted for display on the pie charts below for easy understanding of their contribution to the final destination choice. Factors that have an overall influence of above 50% would be considered in this case. Then using simple arithmetic, each factors overall contribution to a destination decision would be illustrated.

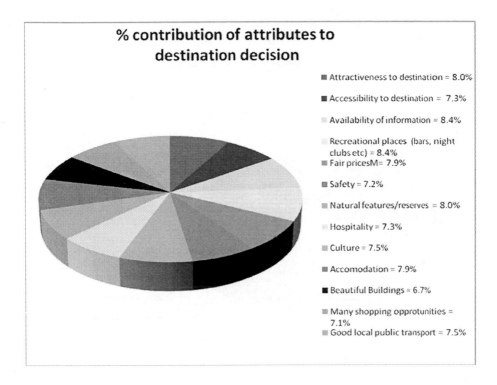

% contribution of attributes to destination decision

- Attractiveness to destination = 8.0%
- Accessibility to destination = 7.3%
- Availability of information = 8.4%
- Recreational places (bars, night clubs etc) = 8.4%
- Fair pricesM = 7.9%
- Safety = 7.2%
- Natural features/reserves = 8.0%
- Hospitality = 7.3%
- Culture = 7.5%
- Accomodation = 7.9%
- Beautiful Buildings = 6.7%
- Many shopping opprotunities = 7.1%
- Good local public transport = 7.5%

Figure 2. Most considered attributes in the destination decision of Gotland Island.

The above pie chat shows the various attributes percentage contribution to a decision on the destination choice for Gotland Island. The history of the place does not have a strong influence on the destination choice as seen from the attributes above. Thus visitors went to wherever they wanted based on other attributes than the history of the destination. This is also evident in Limbe city as illustrated below. Attractiveness of the destination, natural feature /reserves, hospitality and recreational place, availability of information and safety seem to be the attributes with the strongest influence on destination decisions. Almost all attributes considered had an equal impact on the final decision as seen above.

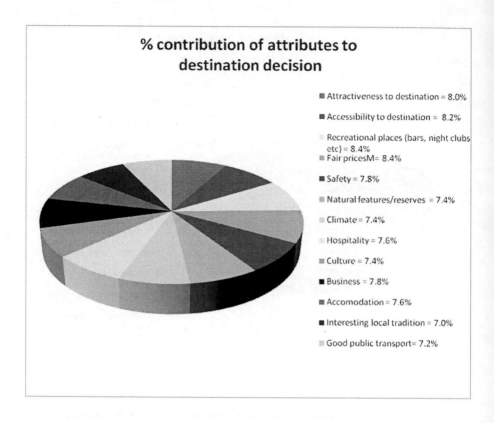

Figure 3. Most considered attributes in the destination decision of Limbe city.

From these pie charts it can be observed that both destinations did not seem to have strict laws or cultures that could hinder visitation, however visitors to Limbe reported a love for the local tradition than visitors to Gotland Island who showed no particular attachment or love for the local tradition of this destination. Both visitors also reported hospitality in these destinations which they considered it has a very strong influence on their destination decision. The climate unfortunately has a great impact on destinations choices. I say unfortunately because climate is unpredictable.

It is also important to note that availability of information which appeared as an attribute in Gotland Island destination decision was absent in Limbe city. I had earlier suggested a reason for its absence, which is prior knowledge about the town as Cameroon citizens. Many shopping opportunities too did not have much of an influence on the decision to visit Limbe city.

Age analysis

According to table 4 and 8, there are almost equal numbers of visitors who are between 15-25 years from Gotland Island and Limbe city. They only vary in the visit frequency to each destination. For the age group 25-35 Gotland had 42% and Limbe 36%. The age group 35-45 was in Gotland higher than Limbe.

But from 45 years and above, there seems to be a wide variation ,that is 8% for Gotland as to 22% for Limbe visitors. Analysing these results on number of visitors in each age group, iI can say that people in between the age group 25-45 are very active and mobile thus it's a good segment for any tourism industry to target. This is because looking at the tables 4 and 8, these combine age groups have the largest number of visitors in each destination.

4.4 A suggestion towards not important attributes

Looking at both results it is clear that the history of place has no strong influence visitor's choice of destinations to visit considering Gotland Island and Limbe city. Climate does not have a very strong influence on destination decisions in Gotland Island, and in Limbe it had a mean of only 3.7 (just 0.2 above 3.5 which was considered significant because at least 50% of respondents rated it). This support studies by Hamilton et al, (2005) concerning weather.

4.5 Criticism of this study

This research which seeks to explain a global phenomenon on factors that prompt a visitor to choose a particular destination is being carried out only in two strategic destinations. Although these regions could give a clear cut reason why visitors are motivated toward particular destinations, the results may not however be representative enough to provide all the necessary facts that prompt the choosing of a particular destination.

Respondents however may alter their answers for personal reasons, prestige, to protect town's image.

Also the variables used to investigate this study could be too small since many other factors can be advanced to measure what makes a destination ideal for a visit.

The sample size could be small, whereas a bigger number of respondents could give various diverse reason which could be use to draw up conclusions.

Time was also an issue because to convince a respondent to take time out of their tight schedule to fill in this questionnaire is not easy. They could hastily just answer the questions without reflecting to provide real responses. Besides some were done only via email and respondents may decide to do it only at their own time.

There was also a language barrier especially with visitors to Gotland Island since most of them are Swedish speakers and I am English speaking. I had to explain in English with demonstrations to clear some doubts about some attributes in visitors minds especially concerning their personal opinions or reasons for choosing Gotland Island.

Some attributes too like service tangibility could not be measure since they are quite intangible and can only be measured using tangible objects as Clow et al. (2006, p. 404) suggested. This could lead to a shift in the intended attribute to be measured.

5.0 Conclusion

From this research I conducted, testing the formulated hypothesis and using only a quantitative research as Fitzpatrick et al, (1998) suggested, I can conclude that there are some significant factors that trigger visitors to choose a particular. There is striking evidence that the development of a country and visitor's personal exposure to diverse ideas has a strong drive towards destination choices. This research being done in developed and a developing country produces these facts.

Gotland Island is a town in a developed country and it visitors seem to appreciate quality. This is seen as they are not too objective about prices in their destination choices. They search for information on the internet before travelling. This search of information goes a long way to create awareness about destinations. Knowledge is acquired in the process thus ideas or images are built in this process of information search therefore their destination choices would undergo a lot of scrutiny to qualify them as a potential place for visit.

For the fact that many more visitors arrive to Gotland Island mostly in the summer and I could still get some even now, shows visitors consider other variable besides the weather, which they have already discovered in this particular destination and they would use these attribute criteria to evaluate any other destination they ever consider visiting. They also appreciate comfort as considering good public transport.

On the other hand visitors to Limbe city as we have seen have different attributes they consider more important besides those chosen by visitors of Gotland Island. Limbe visitors here appreciate convenience and depend on one another through word of mouth for destination choices while Gotland Island visitors choose word of mouse. Therefore to actually determine what triggers visitors to choose a particular destination, we would have to consider their culture, awareness and exposure to modern technology. However some attributes used in this research to test their influence on destination choices proved irrelevant like history of the place.

Visitor's gender should always be regarded in any destination decision to know about price sensitivity and attitude toward risk. These are minute points which on the outside we could ignore as having an impact on destination choices but this research has shown that a final decision on the destination to visit whether for leisure, business or any other reason is dependent on a collection of factors.

From this research studies, I can make a final conclusion that visitors in developed countries are prompted by different attributes in their destination choices and visitors in developing countries are also triggered by different attributes. But overall there exist general attributes which are common in any visitor's destination choices. These general attributes include attractiveness of the destination, accessibility to the destination, safety, recreational activities, climate, hospitality, culture, accommodation, and beautiful buildings. These attributes are what Echtner and Ritchie (1993) recommended.

5.1 Researcher's personal opinion

The main aim of this research was to evaluate if visitors consider some attributes before going to any destination. I was particularly interested in this topic because people are constantly travelling from one place to another, and I am also one of them. When we go to sea port, airports and other means by which people travel we would see thousands of people. It is fascinating to know why people travel and how they decide which place to visit. I have had my answers to these questions by conducting this research I think they are important for any tourism industry in the world today.

Refereference list

Ashley, C. 2005. ˝The Indian Ocean tsunami and tourism.˝ http://www.odi.org.uk/ publications/opinions/33 tsunami tourism jan05. Accessed 08.05.06

Bansal, H., and H. Eiselt., 2004. "Exploratory Research of Tourist Motivations and Planning". *Tourism Management* 25:387–396.

Basala, S., & Klenosky, D., 2001." Travel style preferences for visiting a novel destination: A conjoint investigation across the novelty familiarity continuum". *Journal of Travel Research, November 1, 2001; 40(2): 172 - 182.*

Belk, R.W., & Costa, J.A., 1995. ˝International tourism: An assessment and overview.˝ *Journal of Macro marketing*, 15(2), 33–49.

Bolan, P., Williams L., 2008. "The role of image in service promotion: focusing on the influence of film on consumer choice within tourism." *International Journal of Consumer Studies* 32 (2008) 382–390.

Cho, S. Y., 1991. "The Ugly Koreans are coming?". *Business Korea,* 9(2), 25–31.

Cho,V., 2008. "Linking location attractiveness and tourist intention". *Tourism and Hospitality Research* (2008) 8, 220 – 224.

Clow, K, E., James, K, E., Kranenburg, K, E., and Berry, C,T., 2006. "The relationship of the visual element of an advertisement to service quality expectations and source credibility. *Journal of Services Marketing*, 20, 404–411

Coathup, D. C., 1999. "Dominant actors in international tourism". *International Journal of Contemporary Hospitality Management,* 11(2/3), 69–72.

Crick, M. (1996). ˝Representations of international tourism in the social sciences: Sun, sex, sights, savings, and servility". In Y.Apostolopoulos, S. Leivadi& A.Yiannakis (Eds.), *The sociology of tourism: Theoretical and empirical investigations* (pp. 15–50). London: Routledge.

Decrop, A., 2009. "Destination choice set. An Inductive Longitudinal Approach". *Annals of Tourism Research,* Vol. 37, No. 1, pp. 93–115, 2010

Dhebar, A. 1996. "Speeding High-Tech Producer, Meet the Balking Consumer". *Sloan Management Review* 37(2):37–49.

Echtner, C. M., and B. Ritchie., 1993. "The Measurement of Destination Image: An Empirical Assessment". *Journal of Travel Research*, 31 (4): 3–13.

Echtner C., Ritchie J.R.B., 1991. "The Meaning and Measurement of Destination Image". *The Journal of Tourism Studies*, 2 (2), 2-12.

Fall, L.T. & Knutson, B.J., 2001. "Personal values and media usefulness of mature travelers". *Journal of Hospitality and Leisure Marketing*, 8, 97–111.

Fesenmaier, D. R., & Jeng, J., 2000. ´´Assessing structure in the pleasure trip planning process.´´ *Tourism Analysis, 5, 13–27.*

Fitzpatrick, J.,Wright. J. D., Secrist, J., 1998 "Secrets for successful dissertation." http://books.google.com/books .

Gartner, W. C., 1986. "Temporal Influences on Image Change". *Annals of Tourism Research*, 13 (4): 635–644.

Gartner, W.C., 1993." Image formation process". *Journal of Travel and Tourism Marketing*, **2**, 191–215

Google images., 2010. Available from. http://www.google.com/images

Google, Gotland Island., 2010. Available from. http://www.gotland.net/en/see-and-do

Google, Limbe Cameroon., Available from 2010. http://www.odyssei.com/travel-tips/2942.html

Giuliani, M., 1991. ˝Towards an analysis of mental representations of attachment to the home.˝ *Journal of Architecture and Planning Research, 8*, 133–146.

Gunn, C. A. (1972). *"Vacationscape: Designing Tourist Regions"*. Washington DC: Taylor & Francis/University of Texas.

Hamilton, M. J., Maddison, J. D., Tol, S. J., 2005." Climate change and international tourism: A simulation study". *Global Environmental Change* 15 (2005) 253–266.

Henderson, J. C., 2003. "Managing tourism and Islam in Peninsular Malaysia". *Tourism Management, 24, 447–456.*

Hofstede, G., 1989. "Organizing for cultural diversity". *European Management Journal,* 7(4), 390–397.

Hu, Y., Ritchie, J.R.B., 1993. "Measuring destination attractiveness: a contextual approach". *Journal of Travel Research 32 (2), 25–34.*

Jackson, M. ,2001. "Cultural influences on tourist destination choices of 21pacific rim nations". Paper presented at the CAUTHE national research conference, pp. 166–176.

Jang, H., Seokho L., Sang-Woo L., Sung-kwon H., 2007. "Expanding the individual choice-sets model to couples' honeymoon destination selection process". *Tourism Management* 28 (2007) 1299–1314

Kristine de Valck., Bruggen, H. G., Wierenga, B., 2009. "Virtual communities: A marketing perspective". *Decision Support Systems* 47 (2009) 185–203

Korça, P ., 1998. " Residents perception of tourism in a resort town". *Leisure Sciences*, Jul-Sep1998, Vol. 20 Issue 3, p.193.

Lavidge, R., & Steiner, G., 1961. "A model for predictive measurements of advertising effectiveness". *Journal of Marketing*, 25(October), 59–62.

Leisen, B., 2001. "Image segmentation: the case of a tourism destination". *Journal of Services Marketing,* 15(1), 49–66.

Lew A. A., 1987. "The English-speaking tourist and the attractions of Singapore". *Singap J Trop Geogr* 1987;8(1):44–59.

Lee, S., Scott, D., Kim, H., 2008. "Celebrity fan involvement and destination perceptions". *Annals of Tourism Research*, Vol. 35, No. 3, pp. 809–832, 2008.

Lin, C., Duarte, B. M., Kerstetter D, L., Jing-shoung, H., 2007. " Examining the Role of Cognitive and Affective Image in Predicting Choice Across Natural, Developed, and Theme-Park Destinations". *Journal of Travel Research* 2007; 46; 183.

Lundie, S., Dwyer, L., Forsyth, P., 2007. "Environmental-Economic_Measures_of_Tourism Yield". *Journal of Sustainable Tourism*, 2007, Vol. 15, No. 5, 2007.

Meng, F., Uysa,M., 2008. "Effects of Gender Differences on Perceptions of Destination Attributes, Motivations, and Travel Values: An Examination of a Nature-Based Resort Destination". *Journal of sustainable tourism*, Vol. 16, No. 4, 2008.

McKercher, B., Wong, C., Lau G., 2006. "How tourists consume a destination". *Journal of Business Research 59* (2006) 647–652.

Murphy, L., Mascardo, G., Benckendorff, P., 2007. "Exploring word-of-mouth influences on travel decisions: friends and relatives vs. other travelers". *International Journal of Consumer Studies* ISSN 1470-6423

Nedungadi, P., 1990. "Recall and consumer consideration sets: Influencing choice without altering brand evaluations". *Journal of Consumer Research*, 17, 263–276.

Ng, S., Lee_A., Soutar, G.,2007. "Tourists' intention to visit a country: The impact of cultural distance". *Tourism Management* 28 (2007) 1497–1506.

Papinski, D., Scott, D., Doherty, S. T., 2009. " Exploring the route choice decision-making process: A comparison of planned and observed routes obtained using person-based GPS". *Transportation Research Part F 12 (2009) 347–358.*

Pike, S., 2002. "Destination image analysis—a review of 142 papers from 1973 to 2000". *Tourism Management 23, 541–549*

Robson C., 1993. *Real World Research. A Resource for Social Scientists and Practitioner-Researchers.* Blackwell Publishers Inc.

Roe, D., & Urquhart, P., 2001. ´´Pro-poor tourism: Harnessing the world's largest industry for the world's poor.´´ Opinion paper for World Summit on Sustainable Development, International Institute for Environment and Development, London.

Rokeach, M.,1973. *The nature of human values.* New York: Free Press.

Ryan, C., 2002. "From motivation to assessment". In C. Ryan (Ed.), *The tourist experience* (2nd ed., pp. 58–77). London: Continuum

Solomon M., Bamossy G., Askegaard s., and Hogg. M. K., 2006. *Consumer Behavior: European Perspective,* 3rd edition, Prentice Hall. New Jersey. ISBN 978-0-273-71472-9

Smith, M. C. & Mackay, K. J., 2001. "The organisation of information in memory for pictures of tourist destinations: are there age related differences? ". *Journal of Travel Research*, **39**, 261–266.

Truong T, Henscher D.1985. " Measurement of travel time values and opportunity cost model from a discrete-choice model". *The Econ J* 1985;95:438–51 [June].

Um, S., and J. L. Crompton., 1992. "The Roles of Perceived Inhibitors and Facilitators in Pleasure Travel Destination Decisions". *Journal of Travel Research*, 30 (3): 18–25.

Wong, J., & Yeh, C., 2009. "Tourist hesitation in destination decision making". *Annals of Tourism Research*, Vol. 36, No. 1, pp. 6–23, 2009.

World Trade Organization., 2010. Available from
http://www.unwto.org/aboutwto/why/en/why.php?op=1

Appendix

Questionnaire

Research studies

Good day Sir/ Madame, I am a Masters student at the University of Gotland, Sweden. I am presently conducting a research on the factors that influence visitors to choose a particular destination for a visit. I would be delighted to have your view on these factors, I assure you that response would be treated confidentially. Please take some time now to give your views to the following questions.

A. Pre-visitation
1. How often do you visit Gotland/ Limbe?...

2. How did you hear about this place?..

B. During visitation

Please rate on the scale 1-5 how the following factors influence your visit to this destination.

1- Not at all important, 5- very important.

1. Attractiveness of the place	1 2 3 4 5
2. Accessibility to this destination	1 2 3 4 5
3. Availability of information	1 2 3 4 5
4. Recreational places (bars, night clubs etc)	1 2 3 4 5
5. Fair prices	1 2 3 4 5
6. Safety	1 2 3 4 5
7. Natural feature/ reserves.	1 2 3 4 5
8. Laws of the destination	1 2 3 4 5
9. Unlimited visitation to places in the destination	1 2 3 4 5
10. Climate	1 2 3 4 5
11. Hospitality	1 2 3 4 5
12. Culture (food, drinks, language, religion etc.)	1 2 3 4 5

13. History of the place   1 2 3 4 5

14. Business   1 2 3 4 5

15. Accommodation.   1 2 3 4 5

16. Beautiful buildings   1 2 3 4 5

17. Interesting Local tradition   1 2 3 4 5

18. Many shopping opportunity   1 2 3 4 5

19. Good Local public transport   1 2 3 4 5

20. Any other reason? ....

C. Post visitation.

1. Would you visit this destination again?...

2. Would you recommend this place to another person?............................

D. Demography

1. Occupation...

2. Age   15-25 ☐   25-35 ☐   35-45 ☐   45$^+$ ☐

3. Gender   ☐   Male   ☐   Female

4. Nationality..

Thank you for your time. I again want to assure that this questionnaire would be treated with confidentiality.

Scientific Publishing House

offers

free of charge publication

of current academic research papers, Bachelor´s Theses, Master's Theses, Dissertations or Scientific Monographs

If you have written a thesis which satisfies high content as well as formal demands, and you are interested in a remunerated publication of your work, please send an e-mail with some initial information about yourself and your work to *info@vdm-publishing-house.com*.

Our editorial office will get in touch with you shortly.

VDM Publishing House Ltd.
Meldrum Court 17.
Beau Bassin
Mauritius
www.vdm-publishing-house.com

Printed by
Schaltungsdienst Lange o.H.G., Berlin